I0816040

PRAYING WITH SAINT NICHOLAS

25 DAILY READINGS

PRAYING WITH

AD 270 **SAINT NICHOLAS** AD 343

PRAYING WITH SAINT NICHOLAS

A CHRISTMAS DEVOTIONAL

MATT MIKALATOS

A Tyndale nonfiction imprint

Visit Tyndale online at tyndale.com.

Visit Tyndale Momentum online at tyndalemomentum.com.

Visit the author online at www.Mikalatos.com.

Praying with Saint Nicholas: A Christmas Devotional

Cover designed by Ron C. Kaufmann

Interior designed by Laura Cruise

Edited by Deborah King

The author is represented by Ambassador Literary, Nashville, TN.

ISBN 978-1-4964-5126-2

Printed in China

31 30 29 28 27 26 25
7 6 5 4 3 2 1

To Myca, Allie, Zoey, and Krista, who had to listen to me share new things I was learning about Nicholas for over a year. It was so often that you started saying "#SantaFacts" whenever I shared a new one. I am deeply thankful for the blessing you are in my life.

Contents

Introduction

Christmas is my favorite holiday.

I know, I know, it's too commercial, and the pressure of making it perfect can be stressful, and yes, so-and-so is never satisfied with their gifts, and candy canes look better than they taste.

But I love—have always loved—Christmas. Not only because of the carefully wrapped presents and the jolly lights, the loving family, the parties, the singing. I love Christmas because I'm hungry for miracles.

I want angels appearing in the dark, visions and dreams and a star in the east that tells the wise, "A great king is born!" I want to see Jesus, wrapped in cloths, lying in his mother's arms, the newborn who existed before creation, choosing to pitch a tent next to ours for a while.

And I want the simpler miracles too: armies putting down their guns on Christmas Eve, or a stranger helping someone in need find shelter, or just adults tucking kids into bed and saying, "Tomorrow something wonderful is going to happen," and then working hard to create wonder.

And, yes, I love Santa Claus. Or, as we sometimes call him, Saint Nicholas. Honestly, I knew a lot more about the jolly elf who magically flies around the world in one evening than about the historical person he's based on. Still, I thought I had a pretty good idea of who the historical Nicholas was: he had thrown some gold in a window or down a chimney or something like that, he was a leader in the church, and he also loved Christmas.

But as I researched Saint Nicholas—the history, the myths, the legends—I found myself deeply moved by a story that was completely foreign to me. I had heard little bits before, but seeing it all together painted the portrait of a man I found not just interesting but inspiring. My respect grew from "He's the guy who loves Christmas" to "How can I be more like Nicholas in my daily life?"

He was someone hungry for miracles too. He paid attention to the people around him and asked how he could help. If they needed money, or a protector, or a prayer, Nicholas provided it for them as a servant of God. He became God's miracle for them.

Christmas as we know it—the religious celebration of the birth of Christ—didn't even exist until the last few years of Nicholas's life. But as I got to know this man better, I understood why we've come to associate him with Christmas. He loved children. He loved to give gifts. He spent several years living near Bethlehem. He couldn't help but keep turning his attention to the most vulnerable people in his world: children, single women, the poor.

There are few other believers in the history of the church who have become so universally beloved in the Christian community (and beyond). And while there are amazing legends and myths and exaggerations that eventually lead us to a jolly old elf at the North Pole handing out gifts for Christmas, all of this started from a single seed of truth: a man who loved Jesus, and loved people, and dedicated his life to bringing gifts to the needy.

Sorting the history from the myths takes a lot of work, so I've included a section in the back if you're interested to make it clearer what we "know" to be true and what we suspect might be true about Nicholas. We don't have any contemporary writings of Nicholas . . . no notes, no sermons, not even a letter written between him and a friend. So what we do know about him comes from oral history and writings about him, mostly composed after his death.

We do know this: Nicholas was born on the coast of the Mediterranean, in a town called Patara. It was March 15, the last days of winter, AD 270. We know his parents died when he was young and that he gave away his wealth to help people in need. Because his bones are still preserved in Bari, Italy, we know that he had his nose broken at some point, and that he suffered horrific arthritis in his later years.

In this book we'll reflect on Nicholas's life and pray for God to give us insights that will bring us more deeply into the Christmas season and help us be transformed to see the world through God's eyes, just as Nicholas worked to do. There are purposely twenty-five entries, designed so that if you start reading daily on December 1, the book will take you right through to Christmas Day. But honestly, while Nicholas has become synonymous with Christmas today, his life and his example is something we can all apply to our everyday lives, regardless of the season. So I hope you will read and enjoy these devotions other times of the year as well.

Here's my prayer for all the readers of this book:

Lord God, whether we consider these words at Christmas or some other time of the year, give us your heart as we read. Give us a deep desire for the "peace on earth" your angels proclaimed, and show us the light that comes to those who have walked in darkness. As we look at Nicholas, a man who loved you and the people around him deeply, let us be inspired by his person and life. Make us more like Nicholas and more like you. Amen.

PART ONE

NICHOLAS OF PATARA

Nicholas was born in Patara, the capital city of a Roman province called Lycia and Pamphylia. This area is part of modern-day Turkey. Patara was a wealthy seaport, an important city, and a nexus of multiple cultures coming together to trade and live.

So don't imagine Nicholas in the frozen wastes of the North Pole. He grew up on the coast of the Mediterranean Sea and swam in those warm waters from a young age. He may have eaten olives and cheese and bread for breakfast and run with his friends through the city's paved streets and past the impressive stone gates and temples to Artemis of the Ephesians and to Apollo (in fact, it was said that Apollo's son, Patarus, founded the city).

Nicholas's family was Greek and wealthy. They were likely well networked among the upper class of the city, which included many other Greek families, as well as Roman merchants and traders. Nicholas was well educated and would have been at least bilingual, speaking and writing in both Greek and Latin.

Nicholas's family were devoted Christians, a religious minority in the empire at the time. In fact, his uncle (also named Nicholas) was a priest. Young Nicholas was well loved, and he lived a happy life beside the sea.

1

A PRAYER FOR THE FUTURE

God can do anything, you know—far more than you could ever imagine or guess or request in your wildest dreams!

EPHESIANS 3:20, MSG

Theophanes and Nona had everything a person could want. A loving relationship. A deep spiritual life. A high social standing and the respect of the city. More money than they could spend in their lifetime.

But they wrestled with unhappiness and dissatisfaction. They wanted, more than anything, a child of their own. They prayed for a child, but their prayers, it seemed, went unanswered, even when they promised God that they would dedicate their child to God's service.

Worried that their hearts might become hardened by this unanswered prayer, Theophanes and Nona started a practice that would become a habit of their lives: they began to seek out the poor and downtrodden of the town and provide for them. If they couldn't have a child, at least they could care for those around them.

As they turned their lives toward the poor, they found that their sadness about not having a child lessened over time. When Nona did become pregnant, they were surprised, shocked, and overjoyed. They immediately made good on the promises they had made in their prayers. They named the boy Nicholas after the local Christian abbot (who was either Theophanes's or Nona's brother, we're not sure which), with the idea that young Nicholas, like his uncle, would grow into a man who dedicated his entire life to God.

Each of these women held a child in their arms who would change the world for the better.

Theophanes and Nona had no way to know just how much their prayers and their child would bless other people. They hadn't prayed for a saint. They hadn't prayed for their child to be a man who would bless people for centuries to come or for their son to become a symbol of God's love for children and of the promises of Christmas.

But that's what God did. Something far more than they asked for: more than they could think to hope or imagine. As they held their infant son, no doubt they thought of two other women who had children when they thought they could not: Mary, the mother of Jesus, and Elizabeth, the mother of John the Baptist.

Each of these women held a child in their arms who would change the world for the better. What an amazing gift to all of us!

Lord God, I know that I can't tell the future, or even guess at the wonderful and amazing things you may do in the world in the days to come, let alone the years to come. Give me the courage to pray for amazing, even impossible, things, knowing that you may choose to do something even better than I could think to ask.

2

A PRAYER FOR LIGHT IN TIMES OF DARKNESS

The people walking in darkness have seen a great light; on those living in the land of deep darkness a light has dawned.

ISAIAH 9:2

In the time and place where Nicholas grew up, December 25 was a big deal. It was one of the biggest festival days of the year, called *Dies Natalis Solis Invicti* (Latin for "Birthday of the Invincible Sun"). When Nicholas was four years old, the emperor Aurelius made this day an official national holiday throughout the empire.

Sol Invictus, the invincible or unconquered sun, was a sun deity who appeared on Roman coins. He was celebrated on December 25 because in the Roman calendar that was the date of the winter solstice (the longest night of the year). When Sol Invictus was "born" every year, the sun beat back darkness and brought spring and summer with him.

It's interesting to think that December 25, which would become so deeply entwined with both the birth of Jesus and

Nicholas and his family knew something beautiful, that the end of winter and the coming of spring was nothing compared to humanity's deep darkness that was overcome with the birth of the Savior of the world, the Messiah, our Lord Jesus Christ.

the story of Nicholas, was a completely different holy day when Nicholas was a child: a celebration of a god Nicholas never acknowledged and a religious system he was in opposition to.

Christians in those days started to talk about Jesus in terms that would put him in opposition to the Roman sun god Sol Invictus. They called Jesus the "Sun of Righteousness." Eventually, Jesus took over the invincible sun god completely, taking his birthday and proving Sol Invictus was not quite invincible after all.

It's important to understand that for Nicholas, he lived as a religious minority in a city that still had temples to Apollo and Artemis. Christians were looked down on and even blamed for the city's trouble. As a kid, no doubt Nicholas faced some teasing or possibly worse from his peers for the strange person he worshiped: a backwater man from some nowhere corner of the empire who claimed to be God and then was crucified. Nicholas, of course, believed that Jesus had then risen from the dead, a story that sounded ridiculous to many people then, just as it does today.

But Nicholas and his family knew something beautiful, that the end of winter and the coming of spring was nothing compared to humanity's deep darkness that was overcome with the birth of the Savior of the world, the Messiah, our Lord Jesus Christ.

Jesus, help me to prepare my heart for the celebration of your birth. We were in darkness in so many ways, and you brought light to our lives. Even the smallest light overcomes the darkness. Teach me to look for your spark in the darkest places. Help me to see you clearly in the days ahead.

3

A PRAYER IN TIMES OF LOSS

The Lord is close to the brokenhearted
and saves those who are crushed in spirit.

PSALM 34:18

Nicholas's parents were sick.

It was no great surprise, lots of people were sick. A plague was spreading throughout the empire, and people were dying, many of them alone as loved ones abandoned them, afraid of catching the plague themselves.

His parents had never been people to turn their back on the poor or suffering. In fact, many in the Christian community set aside their own safety to take care of their neighbors. It was only a matter of time before his parents would fall victim to the disease.

Nicholas wore out his knees praying for his parents, begging God to spare them. But in the end Nona and Theophanes both died, leaving their teenage son alone. Nicholas was stunned by the loss. Orphaned, his heart broken, and surrounded by many people experiencing the same type of loss, Nicholas felt himself sinking into despair.

The lives of saints are often touched by sorrow, and Nicholas was no exception. Like any person, he wrestled with the pain, the loss, and questions about God's choices in that moment . . . about why God didn't heal his parents.

Nicholas found that when he turned his attention toward those who were suffering, when he tried to find a way to help them, his own grief lifted a bit.

And yet, Nicholas couldn't deny that when he prayed, he felt—not every day, but some days—a strong and comforting presence, breathing peace and comfort into his soul.

In his best moments, Nicholas could see beyond himself to the many other people who were suffering in the city. Not just those who were sick, but people like himself who had lost their families, people struggling to make a living as their chief breadwinners grew ill or died. Nicholas found that when he turned his attention toward those who were suffering, when he tried to find a way to help them, his own grief lifted a bit.

He felt that by helping others he could honor his parents, honor his faith, and honor God. His own lifelong habit of service to the poor and suffering began here, in his darkest moment of deep loss.

God, you have promised to be near when I am brokenhearted. You have promised comfort for those who are grieving. I claim those promises now, as painful and difficult as it is to hope for something more than pain and suffering. I pray that you would help me turn toward others who are experiencing loss. Use my own suffering to give me insight and strength to comfort those around me when the time is right.

4

A PRAYER FOR WHEN WE ARE DEFENSELESS

Defend the weak and the fatherless; uphold the cause of the poor and the oppressed. Rescue the weak and the needy; deliver them from the hand of the wicked.

PSALM 82:3-4

Imagine for a moment the terror Nicholas must have felt. His parents—both of them—had succumbed to a terrible illness. They had died within days of each other. He must have felt adrift, lost, lonely.

He had grown up—to this point—with everything a boy could want. Loving parents. Wealth. An extended community that deeply loved his parents and thus loved him as well. Yet all around him there were many people in poverty, many people suffering, many people at risk of losing everything, and for the first time in his life Nicholas truly understood that to the core of his being.

In fact, unlike so many others who found themselves orphaned in these years of upheaval, Nicholas had a community. He had other family too. He had money.

There were children on the street with none of those things. There were families who had lost their homes, parents who had sold their children so that at least they would all have food to eat. Nicholas himself had visited fatherless children or delivered food to widows with his parents. It was strange, now, to find himself on the other end of that equation. Now he was the orphan, he was the one waking in the night crying, he was the one filled with a terrible, haunting loneliness. He was afraid that this might be how he would feel for the rest of his life.

He would not be completely alone for long. His uncle Nicholas lived in town, and was, in fact, a priest. He was the bishop of Patara and had even founded a monastery called New Zion. He would have been one of the first to find Nicholas after Theophanes and Nona died . . . it wouldn't be surprising for Bishop Nicholas to be at the bedside of his loved ones when they passed, for that matter.

No doubt he comforted the boy who had been named after him, put his arm around Nicholas's shoulder, shared one of the many Scriptures that speak about God's deep love and promises to care for those who have lost their parents. Maybe he even told him the story from the Gospel of John, when Jesus is leaving his followers and promises them, "I will not leave you as orphans; I will come to you."

Nicholas grabbed that promise and held on tight: God would never leave him completely alone. Jesus left his followers but sent a Comforter and Teacher in the Holy Spirit. And more than that, Jesus promised to return someday himself as well.

Nicholas learned to expect God's presence in his most difficult moments. He would not be disappointed.

God, in this moment of profound loss and loneliness I feel defenseless. I am afraid of what the future holds. Remind me of your goodness. Remind me of your promise never to leave us as orphans. Send me your comfort and peace, and assure me that you will send daily bread for all my needs.

5

A PRAYER FOR STRENGTH TO FOLLOW WHOLEHEARTEDLY

Jesus looked at him and loved him. "One thing you lack," he said. "Go, sell everything you have and give to the poor, and you will have treasure in heaven. Then come, follow me."

MARK 10:21

It wouldn't have been wrong for Nicholas to keep the money. His parents had earned it, after all, and they had left it to him. There was an argument to be made that keeping the money would be better for everyone in the long run. After all, his parents had trained him how to use it. They had shown him how to use wealth for the betterment of the people around them. They had always been generous, had always been focused on the needs and well-being of their community. He should keep the money, maybe, and make more.

But Nicholas was haunted by the idea that maybe, just maybe, Jesus meant what he said to the rich young man in Scripture: sell everything. Get rid of all your worldly possessions. And it would make sense then to take that money and give it to the community of faith to watch over and hand out as appropriate. Perhaps he should just give the money to the church.

But that's not what Jesus said. He said to sell everything and then give the money to the poor. Not keep it for himself. Not even turn it over to the church. See those in need and use the money you've gained to meet those needs. Trust that the poor know what they need better than you know, and that with the money they can do what is best for themselves and their families.

There must have been an enormous temptation to serve God in a different way. Yes, there were people suffering all around him, but wasn't he suffering too? He'd just lost his parents, and now he was going to sell their house? Sell their property? Mother's jewelry, father's horses, the mansion he'd grown up in? All of that gone, replaced with what?

Bread for the poor. Empty bellies full for a time, the sick able to see a doctor, a child given a new blanket, a family on the brink of poverty pulled back from the edge. When he thought of it that way, he felt something lift from his shoulders. A lightness came over him. It felt less like a sacrifice and more like a service.

He would soon learn that this sort of service suited him. He devoted his life to giving beautiful gifts to other people.

Jesus, I am tempted sometimes to explain away your words and your teachings, especially the ones that are most costly. There are days when I am glad to follow you, so long as you don't ask anything more of me. It's when you ask for the difficult—or the impossible—that I start to suspect I must have misheard you and I look for less challenging things you might have meant. Teach me to follow you with my whole heart, holding nothing back. Let me enter into the joy of pure service to you.

6

A PRAYER FOR THE CHILDREN OF THE WORLD

Let the little children come to me, and do not hinder them, for the kingdom of God belongs to such as these.

MARK 10:14

Nicholas loved children, and every story, every tradition agrees with this. Maybe it's because he was a child himself when he was launched out into the world as an orphan. Or maybe it's because he—like Jesus—saw the Kingdom of Heaven so clearly in their lives.

No matter where Nicholas went in his travels—whether around the city of Patara or, later in life, to Egypt, Bethlehem, or Nicaea—he showed special care for kids. He paid attention to them. He gave them little gifts. Nicholas made children feel seen, and he let them know they were loved.

Over the centuries we turned this love of children into a story about a man who spends his year making gifts to magically deliver on Christmas Day, and there is a certain charm and beauty to that story. But I can't help but think there is something even more beautiful about an ordinary man who made sure his pockets were full of gifts, who walked among the children every day, who stooped down to them and talked about their days. A man who stopped to look at a lizard with a child, who listened as they told him about their everyday troubles and in the end handed them a piece of candy or a small trinket, a souvenir of meeting an adult who was safe, who loved them, who would watch out for them and cared about their lives.

Nicholas made children feel seen, and he let them know they were loved.

In some countries, Saint Nicholas is celebrated on December 6 in honor of the day that he passed away. Children are given special cookies, or candy, or small gifts. The kids, excited for his arrival, may leave out grass or carrots for his donkey.

They go to bed, whispering to each other, "Saint Nicholas is coming!" and in the morning they find presents under their pillows, in their shoes, squirreled away in their socks. There might be oranges, or chocolate coins, or other sweet treats.

All because over a thousand years ago there was a man who loved Jesus and loved children so much that he became known for it, among the children as well as the adults. Wouldn't it be amazing if children today knew a person of peace in the church who made them feel welcomed, loved, and safe? What a gift that would be!

I'm reminded that when the children were brought to Jesus, some adults tried to send them away. Children are so often trouble from an adult's point of view. They don't follow the rules. They squirm and fight and talk too loud and don't pay attention to the things adults think they should. But Jesus took the children in his arms and blessed them. And he told us the Kingdom of God belongs to children!

Lord God, I pray for the children of the world—wherever they are, whatever their faith or lack of faith, whatever their situation, whether it be plenty or famine or peace or war—and I pray your blessing on them. Let the children come to you and find blessing. And let me, as one of your servants, be a person who loves children, who brings them gifts and blessing and peace and a safe place in the world.

7

A PRAYER TO BE A BLESSING

When you give to the needy, do not let your left hand know what your right hand is doing, so that your giving may be in secret. Then your Father, who sees what is done in secret, will reward you.

MATTHEW 6:3-4

Maybe the most famous story of Nicholas, and one that still influences how many of us celebrate Christmas to this day, is the story of the three bags of gold.

It goes like this: There was a man who had three daughters. He had once been rich, but because of the changing fortunes of the day, his family had fallen into abject poverty. He didn't have the money to pay for his daughters to get married. And in the meantime, he worried that his household didn't even have enough to buy food.

In a moment of desperation, he decided that he would have to sell his daughters into sexual slavery. As horrific as this would be for each of them, at least they would have something to eat. At least they would live.

Nicholas heard about the man's plans, and that very night he snuck to the man's house and threw a bag of gold coins through the window. (Or—as the story was told across cultures and generations—he threw the gold down the chimney, or he placed it in their shoes, or he dropped it into their stockings that hung on the fireplace.)

In the morning, the whole family rejoiced, because it was enough money for the eldest daughter to be married into a safe and reputable household. What a great blessing!

The second night, once again, Nicholas slipped through the darkness and, while everyone else was sleeping, threw a bag of gold coins through the window. The next morning, once again, the whole house rejoiced, for the second daughter would be spared from slavery.

The third night, the man knew what was coming. He was deeply thankful to whoever was throwing gold through the window—how could he not be?—and was determined to find them and thank them.

The moment the gold coins sailed through his window and hit the floor, the man burst out his door and caught the family's secret benefactor. He recognized him at once. "Nicholas! It was you giving us this money?"

Nicholas was embarrassed. He didn't want any credit for his good deed, and he didn't want any thanks for it either. He took the man's arms and said, "Thank God alone for these gifts. They've come in answer to your prayers!"

Lord, teach me to see two things clearly: how much you have blessed me with and the needs of the people around me. Give me courage to use my blessings to meet their needs, so that your gifts to me can become a blessing to them too.

PART TWO

NICHOLAS, BISHOP OF MYRA

Myra was an important city in the region Nicholas grew up in . . . about fifty miles from Patara, where Nicholas was born. Myra had a beautiful theater carved from stone that could hold about 11,000 people. The city was well known for its various industries, including a thriving business creating purple dye. Tombs were often carved into the cliffs and made to look like temples. And speaking of temples, there were many. All of the Roman gods were well venerated in Myra, but most especially Artemis of the Ephesians. There was a large synagogue, too, and famous people from around the world had been known to visit, or at least to hang around at the port while changing ships. In fact, Luke the evangelist and Paul the apostle had stopped over in Myra on their way to Rome (Acts 27:5).

We don't know precisely why Nicholas came to Myra. Nicholas had become a priest some years before, so it's possible he came on official duties of some kind. Or, there were Christians there and a Greek community he may have been connected to. Or he could have been following the steps of Paul or visiting a friend. I couldn't find any theories, any ideas of why he may have come to town. Perhaps Nicholas would have just said, "Because God wanted me there."

Regardless, Nicholas became a bishop—the bishop of Myra, in fact—when he was thirty years old. As you will see in the stories to come, he wasn't well known or a person of influence when he arrived, but the local church leaders saw his arrival as a literal answer to prayer.

Nicholas arrived in Myra at the same time that anti-Christian persecution from the government was on the rise. He spent five years—very likely his first five years as a bishop—in prison. During his many years as bishop, Nicholas showed special care to the poor, children, the hungry, and others who had been cast aside in some way.

Nicholas was a spiritual leader in Myra, and eventually a civic leader, too, as the Christian faith grew in influence over the decades. He would remain bishop of Myra for forty-three years, with no scandals, no horrible secrets to uncover, no one to speak out against him.

He was respected and beloved and spent over half his life in this city as the bishop of Myra.

8

A PRAYER FOR OUR LEADERS

Remember your leaders, who spoke the word of God to you. Consider the outcome of their way of life and imitate their faith.

HEBREWS 13:7

The church in Myra was an old one for the young Christian faith. The first bishop, Nicander, had been consecrated before the end of the first century by the saint Titus, a disciple of the apostle Paul. Titus had been Greek, just like Nicholas and his family, and Nicander was one of Titus's converts, along with a man named Hermas. Not long after their conversions, Nicander became bishop, and Hermas became a priest.

These two men saw many people in Myra come to Christ . . . enough so that they drew the attention of the local authorities and found themselves brought before the city prefect, Libanius. He tried to convince them to stop their missionary activities, because their Christian converts did not follow the religious expectations of the empire. When neither bribery nor threats worked on the two men, Libanius ordered them tortured.

Despite multiple horrific tortures, the two men neither recanted nor died. So, in the end, Libanius ordered them buried alive. This was the fate of the Christian leaders of Myra, to be martyred for the faith.

That had been just over two hundred years before Nicholas arrived in Myra, and the Christian community there had only grown in the years since. Now it was the year 300, and the current bishop of Myra had died. The leaders of the church didn't know what to do or who to replace him with. Persecution was rising again in the empire, and to be a bishop held both great responsibility and some danger, so the choice was especially delicate. The bishops were determined to install a new leader with God's seal of approval, not to merely make a pragmatic choice of who might be best.

Grieved at the loss of their friend, several bishops gathered to pray and fast and seek God's will about a replacement. They prayed late into the night.

Around midnight, the most senior of the bishops heard a message from God: the first person to come to the church to pray was the man God had chosen to become the next spiritual leader for the community. The bishops heard this message with great joy, and set themselves near the church doors, excited to see who the Lord would send.

It was not yet dawn when a young man—barely thirty—came to the doors of the church. The senior bishop asked him, "Who are you?" For the bishops didn't know this young priest.

"I am the sinner Nicholas," he said, "the servant of your holiness, master."

The bishops invited him in, and they consecrated him with prayers, installing him as bishop before the sun rose. He would serve this city and the community for the next forty-three years.

Lord God, send us leaders who are humble and kind. May they be people of prayer. When there is persecution, give them strength and wisdom to lead with kindness and courage. When there is peace, let them see more clearly the people in need. And may they serve you and our community for many years, living to an old age, held in honor by your people.

9

A PRAYER FOR WHEN WE FACE PERSECUTION

Blessed are you when people insult you, persecute you and falsely say all kinds of evil against you because of me. Rejoice and be glad, because great is your reward in heaven, for in the same way they persecuted the prophets who were before you.

MATTHEW 5:11-12

Nicholas became bishop of Myra just as persecution against Christians was ramping up again. Diocletian—one of the four emperors at the time, the tetrarch who was in authority over Nicholas's region—wanted to see Rome return to worshiping the traditional gods of the empire.

On February 23, 303—less than three years after Nicholas became bishop—Diocletian released an edict: Christian buildings were to be burned, their treasures seized, and their Scriptures destroyed. Christians could no longer legally gather to worship, and their rights to a fair trial in the courts were removed. Christians in the military were stripped of their rank. Freed Christian slaves would be re-enslaved. And Christian religious leaders were to be thrown in prison.

Diocletian wanted this all done without bloodshed, though there were some who became martyrs while resisting these evil decrees. Overall, the persecution didn't do quite what Diocletian had hoped: break the spirits of the Christians.

Nicholas wouldn't make even a symbolic denial of Christ or pretend to sacrifice to gods he did not believe in.

By November Diocletian offered limited amnesty for Christians, with certain strings attached. Priests could be released from prison if they either recanted Christianity or offered a sacrifice to the Roman gods. There are stories of religious leaders being forced to offer sacrifices or tortured until they agreed to make one.

Diocletian's plan appears to have been to publicize that all the Christian priests had apostatized. He had more trouble with it than he expected.

Tradition tells us that Nicholas was in prison for five years—much longer than the nine months from February to November. The persecution throughout the empire was irregular, and the local authorities differed greatly in how they enforced the law, so it's entirely possible this is true . . . even though Diocletian abdicated his position as emperor in 305.

What we know for sure is this: Nicholas spent a number of years in prison because he refused to deny his faith. Diocletian made it clear that the denial would be largely symbolic: the priests who "denied Christ" went right back to being priests after they were released. Nicholas wouldn't make even a symbolic denial of Christ or pretend to sacrifice to gods he did not believe in.

Lord God, it is so tempting to look at persecution as a punishment, as something to fight. We want to take over the government, boycott companies, denounce celebrities, strike back in some way against those who we perceive to be against us. Teach me to embrace persecution as a blessing. Teach me to accept it with peace and quietness, as you did, and trust that when the time is right you will speak on my behalf.

10

A PRAYER FOR THOSE WHO WOULD HARM US

You have heard that it was said, "Love your neighbor and hate your enemy." But I tell you, love your enemies and pray for those who persecute you, that you may be children of your Father in heaven.

MATTHEW 5:43-45

In the church, we can be quick to label other people as our enemies: People of differing theologies (both inside and outside the church). Politicians. Cultural movers.

And maybe they are our enemies.

If so, Jesus gives us very clear instructions regarding them. We are to love and pray for our enemies. We're supposed to pray for those who seek to harm us because of our faith.

Nicholas knew all about enemies. He had been dragged from his parish and taken to prison, while the authorities burned the Scriptures and took control of their church building. We know from modern evidence that Nicholas had his nose broken at some point in his life. It's likely it was during the five years when he was a prisoner for Christ under Emperor Diocletian. Torture in prison was an ordinary thing at the time, and Diocletian was clear: he wanted ministers to denounce Christ and be returned to their everyday lives as apostates.

There were some ministers who did just that and a few who died during these years. Surely Nicholas would have heard of or even have been friends with Romanus of Antioch, a deacon in the early church. In 302, Romanus stood up during a pagan ritual and denounced all the people who were worshiping idols.

Diocletian—who was trying so hard to get Romans to return to their religious roots—had been there. He ordered Romanus to be burned to death at the stake, but when the soldiers prepared the wood and tied him to the stake, a rainstorm soaked the deacon as well as the wood. Furious, Diocletian ordered his men to cut Romanus's tongue out and throw him in prison.

We are to love and pray for our enemies.

Romanus was tortured for over a year and finally executed in November of 303 . . . perhaps part of the reason Diocletian started offering his limited amnesty. The point all along had been to make a public spectacle of the Christians denouncing their faith and to show the superiority of the Roman gods. But Romanus held up under considerable torture and wouldn't denounce his faith, even in a limited or symbolic way. Diocletian's plan was backfiring, and the public interest in Christianity was growing rather than waning.

Meanwhile, the religious leaders were all being arrested and thrown in prison. A contemporary scholar and historian, Eusebius, says that the prisons were so full of deacons, lectors, priests, and bishops that regular criminals were being pushed out!

As for Nicholas—his sheep scattered, his Scriptures burnt, his nose broken, his friends on the run or imprisoned alongside him—it seems likely that his thoughts would turn toward the Word of God and what it says about dealing with those who would persecute us.

No doubt Nicholas, chained beside his fellow ministers, prayed for Diocletian often.

Jesus, we look to you for our example of how to love our enemies. You didn't condemn those who killed you, but instead asked God to forgive them . . . what they did, they did in ignorance. Help us to see the persecutors through your eyes. And who knows? Perhaps they may be converted from persecutors to followers of Christ. Isn't that how the apostle Paul came into the Kingdom? God, we ask that you bless those who would harm us for following you. Bring them light, revelation, and knowledge of you!

11

A PRAYER FOR THE BROTHERS AND SISTERS

I pray that out of his glorious riches he may strengthen you with power through his Spirit in your inner being, so that Christ may dwell in your hearts through faith.

EPHESIANS 3:16-17

It wasn't enough to destroy the churches, burn the Scriptures, and imprison the ministers. Diocletian wanted more. He wanted the Christian people converted to worshiping the gods of Rome.

In 304 he sent out yet another edict: every person in the region must publicly make a sacrifice to the gods. Those who refused would be executed.

Nicholas and the other imprisoned ministers were horrified. Nicholas knew the temptation of denying God, and most of the leaders of the church were in prison, unable to give advice or comfort to the people as they wrestled with this terrible decision.

We're told that Nicholas prayed for the people during his time in prison, and what he asked God was simple: "Give them strength to keep their faith in you."

No doubt he thought of Paul's prayers that had been lifted up for the people of Ephesus—a city only 250 miles away from where Nicholas was imprisoned—and prayed those words during his long days and longer nights in his prison cell:

> *I pray that out of his glorious riches he may strengthen you with power through his Spirit in your inner being, so that Christ may dwell in your hearts through faith. And I pray that you, being rooted and established in love, may have power, together with all the Lord's holy people, to grasp how wide and long and high and deep is the love of Christ, and to know this love that surpasses knowledge—that you may be filled to the measure of all the fullness of God.*
>
> EPHESIANS 3:16-19

We're told that Nicholas prayed for the people during his time in prison, and what he asked God was simple: "Give them strength to keep their faith in you."

And his prayers were answered: the Christian community stayed strong and even grew during this time of persecution.

And then, suddenly, Diocletian became very ill. He began to abandon his public responsibilities and was hidden away from the public. There were rumors he had died. His less popular edicts (like the one threatening to kill all faithful Christians) went unenforced. When he eventually resurfaced, it was only to announce his retirement to his private estates, where he spent the last few years of his life tending his garden.

As for Bishop Nicholas, he was back among the people, serving them, praying for them, and shepherding them toward Jesus.

God, whatever may come, whatever hardship or persecution—whatever grief or difficulty—give me strength to keep my faith in you. And let me know the depth (and height and width and length) of your love for me and for all humanity.

PART THREE

NICHOLAS IN BETHLEHEM

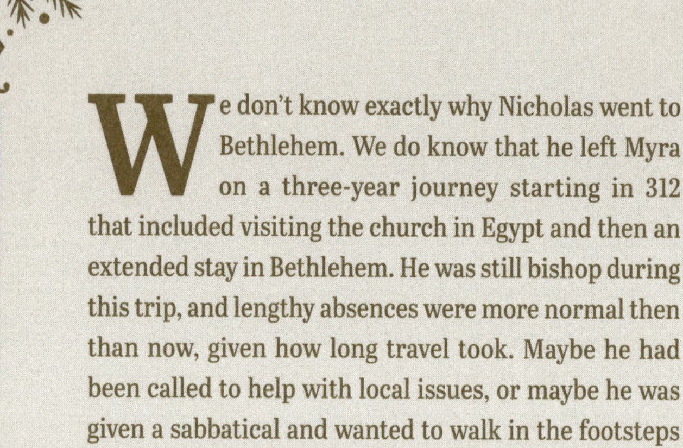

We don't know exactly why Nicholas went to Bethlehem. We do know that he left Myra on a three-year journey starting in 312 that included visiting the church in Egypt and then an extended stay in Bethlehem. He was still bishop during this trip, and lengthy absences were more normal then than now, given how long travel took. Maybe he had been called to help with local issues, or maybe he was given a sabbatical and wanted to walk in the footsteps of Jesus. He could even have been replacing some of the Scriptures and other items the church lost during the Diocletian persecutions. We could come up with a lot of reasons that would make sense.

One thing to recognize was that this area wasn't "the Holy Land" yet.

When Nicholas set out for the place that had once been called Judea, the entire region was called Syria Palestine. In those days, there weren't churches built at every significant historical site of Jesus' life.

There was a cave you could point to and say, "That's the stable where he was born."

There was a hill the locals could point out and say, "There's where he was crucified."

But there weren't cathedrals built over those sites. The age of religious tourism hadn't yet begun . . . though it would start before Nicholas's death, encouraged by Emperor Constantine, who would pour money and attention into the region.

So when you picture Nicholas in Syria Palestine, remember this: he was walking in the footsteps of Jesus, yes, but those steps were largely unmarked. He could sit in the field where Jesus fed the five thousand and not see a single Christian church or monument or sign. He could lean into the tomb with some fellow believers and see that it was empty. He could pray on his knees in the garden of Gethsemane.

But all those places were remembered by words passed down through the generations of saints, guarded by those who remained in the area, and lovingly shared with people like Nicholas, who had come for a short time to be reminded of the physical reality of the God they served.

12

A PRAYER DURING THE STORM

He got up, rebuked the wind and said to the waves, "Quiet! Be still!" Then the wind died down and it was completely calm.

MARK 4:39

In 311 Diocletian—who had Nicholas thrown in prison and persecuted the community of saints—died in his palace, where he had taken up raising cabbages as a hobby. Nicholas had only been bishop for eleven years—half of those spent in prison.

This is the time where tradition tells us that Nicholas left for Syria Palestine. Maybe he needed a spiritual renewal. Or maybe Nicholas felt that with Diocletian dead, his flock would be safe for a while. Regardless, by 312, Nicholas would be headed for the birthplace of Jesus. He would also take time on his journey to visit believers in Egypt.

He set out by boat, and we're told that a huge storm met them on the sea.

There are many times when we find ourselves in the midst of a storm, and like Nicholas, it may even be that the storm comes when we're on our way to try to see Jesus better. It's on the sea headed for Bethlehem that our boat may be in the most danger.

Remember that in those days, a boat, whether small or large, was lovingly crafted by hand, made of wood and rope and cloth. Boats survived the rough seas through ingenuity and prayers and, most importantly, by avoiding storms.

The sailors panicked. They did everything they knew to do: pulled down the sails, rowed into the waves, bailed out the boat, threw the cargo overboard to make the boat lighter. Nothing worked. They were in grave danger, and it seemed likely that the boat was going down.

But Nicholas hadn't done all he could do. He knew the stories, how Jesus had been in a situation just like this. How the sailors had panicked, knowing they would drown, how everyone on the boat was crying out and filled with fear, and Jesus had stood up and rebuked the storm. Told the waves to knock it off. Told the wind to leave them be.

Nicholas said to himself, *Well, it can't hurt to try.* So Nicholas stood up and prayed to God to stop the storm. To everyone's amazement—including Nicholas's—it worked! The wind slipped away. The waves smoothed out. The rain was replaced with the bright and lovely sun.

Nicholas was clear when he talked about this later in life: he didn't stop the storm. God did, in answer to his prayer. But what an amazing moment!

There are many times when we find ourselves in the midst of a storm, and like Nicholas, it may even be that the storm comes when we're on our way to try to see Jesus better. It's on the sea headed for Bethlehem that our boat may be in the most danger.

But Nicholas remembered the example of Jesus and the power of God and asked for peace, and that's precisely what he got.

Jesus, there are times when the waves are crashing over the sides of my boat. The wind howls, and the rain stings my face. I'm afraid that my boat may break to pieces, and then where will I be? Lost at sea, clinging to a piece of wood. And sometimes when I should be focusing on you and the beautiful things you bring, I'm distracted by this terrifying storm of life. So I'm asking, God, can you rebuke the waves? Will you tell the wind to be quiet? Give me the strength to believe that you can answer this prayer. And then, Lord, bless me and everyone on this ship with peace and still waters.

13

A PRAYER FOR GOD'S PRESENCE

The virgin will conceive and give birth to a son, and they will call him Immanuel (which means "God with us").

MATTHEW 1:23

Less than two miles from Bethlehem is a small town called Beit Jala. And in that little town there were monks who had come into possession of a few small houses and a handful of caves. It was in one of these caves that Nicholas lived, we're told, for three years, as he ranged out to walk in the footsteps of Jesus.

He visited all the places you would imagine: the site of Christ's crucifixion, the tomb where they laid his body, the bank of the Jordan River where Jesus was baptized by his cousin. He stood in the place where the Beatitudes were taught. He put his hands in the pool where the paralyzed man waited to be healed. Perhaps he drank from the well where the Samaritan woman drew water. He may have walked down the road to Emmaus, or looked up at the upper room, or prayed in Gethsemane.

But less than two miles away from Nicholas's home base there was a cave, cool and dark, a cave that had once been used as a stable. Twenty years after Nicholas's pilgrimage, a church would be built here. But in Nicholas's day it was just a cave . . . not unlike the one where Nicholas spent his nights. Simple, unadorned, a hole in the rock where God became human and a brilliant light appeared to those who had been walking in darkness.

But here is the miracle that Nicholas dwelled on, meditated on, found himself drawn to over and over: the miracle of "God with us."

Nicholas loved God and he loved children, and here was this strange and wonderful place where those two things intersected in an unexpected way. Here is the place where the eternal God became a human baby, held in his mother's arms, where he was wrapped tight and laid to sleep in a feeding trough.

No doubt Nicholas sometimes reflected on the places where his own story and Jesus' intersected. Like Jesus, he had come to Bethlehem with a mission to serve God and help humanity. And he, too, had left behind his wealth and privilege and power to live in a cave.

In the years to come many stories would be told about Nicholas doing miracles in the town of Beit Jala, even centuries after his death. How Nicholas helped an old woman get out of a locked church, or turned back invaders, or how he appeared in the modern day and caught bombs that threatened the village.

But here is the miracle that Nicholas dwelled on, meditated on, found himself drawn to over and over: the miracle of "God with us." Immanuel, fully God and fully human, coming into the world in this place. A place that could be seen, a cave that could be entered and experienced, a place that could be touched.

Immanuel, you are the God who is with us, whether it's in moments of war, or in a cave, or in those moments when we feel most lost and alone. We don't need to walk in your footsteps in the Holy Land, because you are walking beside us in the places where we live, you are beside us in our everyday lives. Sometimes it's hard to see that you are near. Open our eyes to your presence. Remind us that you are "God with us." Let us see you in this season and in this place.

14

A PRAYER FOR OPEN EYES, OPEN HANDS, AND OPEN HEARTS

Your Father knows what you need before you ask him.

MATTHEW 6:8

In those days of uncertainty, as the empire teetered on the edge of collapse, poverty broke out among the people. We're told there was an elderly couple who had lost nearly everything who were living in a cave, without money for food or even for candles to light the cavern at night. The one luxury that remained from their days of wealth was a beautiful rug, thread worn and half-ruined from life in the cave.

The wife said to her husband, "Take our rug to the market and sell it. Maybe we could get three pieces of gold and buy some food to eat."

The old man said, "We bought it for six gold pieces, but who would pay even a single gold piece for it now?" But these were desperate times, and the man knew he must at least make an attempt to sell the rug.

As he expected, no one at the market gave it a second glance. It was too worn, and he was asking too much for it. At least, that was true until a man named Nicholas came by and looked carefully at the man and the rug.

"What a fine rug," Nicholas said. "Surely you paid more than three gold pieces for it!"

"We paid six, sir, but we have been using it in a cave, and as you can see—though it is still a wonderful rug—it is the worse for wear."

Nicholas laughed. "I myself have need for a cave rug and will gladly pay you six pieces of gold for this small luxury."

The old man thought it was a trick, but the gentleman rolled up the rug, threw it over his shoulder, and dropped six gold pieces into the old man's hand. Then, smiling, he disappeared into the crowd.

The man spent the rest of the day buying food and oil, wine and candles, and hurried home to show his wife their good fortune. But when he arrived, she was angry, and before he could even tell her about the day, she pointed out the rug—their rug!—on the floor of the cave. "I told you to sell this rug, and a man named Nicholas said you had sent him to return it to me!"

The man, astonished, then told her all that had happened and together they ate and drank by candlelight, and praised God for Nicholas and the miracle of the rug.

It is no miracle, Lord, that you see our needs or that you provide for them, because you see everything and you want to give us what is good. But there is a kind of miracle that can come when we learn to see what you see, and when our heart desires what your heart does. Open my eyes to see those in need around me. Open my hands so that I don't hold back what you've entrusted to me. And open my heart so that even what rewards I receive in your service might result in more gifts for the needy people you reveal to me.

15

A PRAYER TO BE LIKE BETHLEHEM

You, Bethlehem Ephrathah, though you are small among the clans of Judah, out of you will come for me one who will be ruler over Israel, whose origins are from of old, from ancient times.

MICAH 5:2

Nicholas lived and served in Beit Jala near Bethlehem for three years. Given the nature of the world he lived in and how leaders in the world were chosen, it's natural to think he might have reflected on how the God of the universe followed a different script.

In the empire, leaders were fighting and squabbling with one another, tearing at each other with words and swords, doing everything they could to gain more power, more influence, and more followers. Their rulers were hardened men of war, soldiers who seized power . . . or politicians who turned secrets to their advantage, liars and manipulators.

But here in Bethlehem something different had taken place. God had sent his only Son as an infant—powerless, reliant on human beings to feed and shelter him. The king of Judah, the

The king of Judah, the king of Israel, the king of the world, born in a humble little town, to a humble little family, in a humble little cave.

king of Israel, the king of the world, born in a humble little town, to a humble little family, in a humble little cave.

Did Nicholas dwell on this, think about it, let it sink deep into his heart and inform the way he thought about leadership? From what we know of how he used his positions of authority later in life, it seems that he did.

"Blessed are the meek, for they will inherit the earth" (Matthew 5:5). Nicholas knew that it wasn't the men of hard words and bloody hands who would rule the world, not in the long run. And it was this little child, the God who humbled himself, who would ride meekly into Jerusalem on a donkey as the crowds shouted, "Save us now!"

How different from the way the world thought about leadership. God chose a small, insignificant place and an unknown family, and he chose that backwater town and a young, unmarried woman as central players in the most important birth in the history of humanity.

Nicholas learned how to keep himself small, how to be humble so that God would do great things in the world around him.

God, make me small. Make me humble. Teach me to be like Bethlehem . . . unremarkable except for the things that you do within me and through me. Teach me not to strive after worldly power but to be content with the power that you provide in my life.

PART FOUR

NICHOLAS AT NICAEA

The Council at Nicaea was the first "ecumenical" gathering of the church. Ecumenical is a word that came from the Greek word "oikoumenikos". . . a word that means, more or less, "the whole inhabited world."

And that's precisely what Emperor Constantine intended when he called for the council, which convened from May to July of 325. Constantine had already shown favor toward the Christians before this. While it was Maxentius who commanded "full religious toleration" in 306, and Galerius who ended Christian persecution in the East in 311, Constantine and Licinius signed the Edict of Milan in 313, giving Christianity legal status in the empire. The Christian faith had continued to flourish as it moved from underground.

Constantine became the singular leader of the empire in 324, and he wanted all the Christian leaders to get together and hash out their disagreements and make sure everyone was on the same page. And there was one disagreement—about whether Jesus had always existed as God or been made by God—that was causing division, especially in the Eastern regions of the church. Constantine wanted to make sure this didn't tear apart his newly reunited Roman Empire.

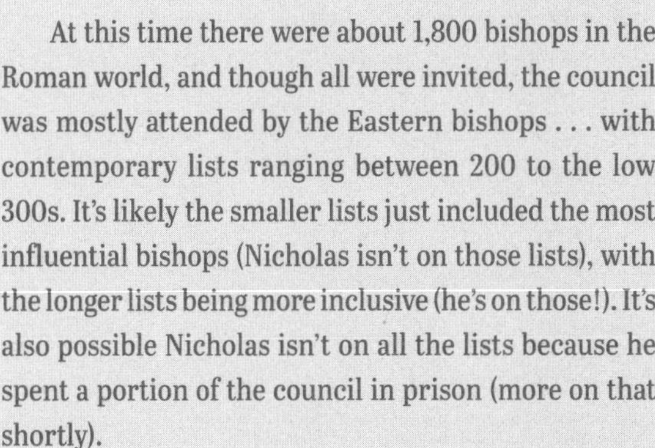

At this time there were about 1,800 bishops in the Roman world, and though all were invited, the council was mostly attended by the Eastern bishops . . . with contemporary lists ranging between 200 to the low 300s. It's likely the smaller lists just included the most influential bishops (Nicholas isn't on those lists), with the longer lists being more inclusive (he's on those!). It's also possible Nicholas isn't on all the lists because he spent a portion of the council in prison (more on that shortly).

The council was held in Nicaea, near the newly established capital, Constantinople. It was a journey of some 400 miles for Nicholas.

Constantine himself attended much of the council, and he planned to enforce the bishops' conclusions with the power of the Roman state. The wide-ranging conversations covered everything from the best dates for Easter to how baptisms should be performed to the most important question of all: Who exactly is Jesus?

16

A PRAYER AGAINST SPIRITUAL ADVERSARIES

*Our struggle is not against flesh and blood,
but against the rulers, against the authorities,
against the powers of this dark world and against
the spiritual forces of evil in the heavenly realms.*

EPHESIANS 6:12

After three years in Syria Palestine, Nicholas came home to Myra. It was a time of great change. Emperor Constantine had started publicly talking about his own conversion to Christianity. In 313—while Nicholas was still in a cave near Bethlehem—the Edict of Milan had made Christianity legal again.

The city of Myra was well known for its temples, including a huge and beautiful one to Artemis Eleuthera, also called Artemis of the Ephesians. This temple was called the most beautiful building in Lycia, the province in which Myra sat, and the territory that Bishop Nicholas oversaw.

It's said that Nicholas had a particularly strong adversarial relationship with the cult of Artemis. He saw the rituals and practices of the temple as a kind of spiritual slavery, and in early stories he calls the temple demonic. The temple had a powerful spiritual presence in his city, and Nicholas saw his people suffering under a false religious power.

The temple of Artemis in Myra had been previously destroyed and then rebuilt around 141, so even the "new" temple was over 150 years by the time of Nicholas. Temples to Artemis stood throughout Asia Minor, and the idea that people would turn away from her must have been unthinkable. She had been worshiped in this area for centuries.

And yet . . . in the years of Nicholas's service, Christianity went from a looked-down-upon cult to the spiritual center of all of Myra, all of Lycia, and indeed, the entire Roman empire. And Artemis—the invincible goddess—went from being universally worshiped at her temple to a god with no followers, her temple destroyed . . . not a stone upon another stone, no building at all.

It's said that Nicholas himself oversaw Artemis's temple being torn down, and that he battled the spiritual forces that had headquartered there, praying for God to protect the people from the spirits, which wished to do them harm.

God, when spiritual forces seem overwhelming—ancient, powerful, unstoppable—remind us that you are still more ancient, still more powerful, and that you can and will destroy spiritual forces that mean to harm us. We pray not only for protection but for victory over those spirits. Tear down their temples, and free those who are in captivity to them.

17

A PRAYER FOR FORGIVENESS

Forgive us our debts, as we also have forgiven our debtors.
And lead us not into temptation, but deliver us from the evil one.

MATTHEW 6:12-13

Nicholas had been back in Myra, serving as bishop, for close to a decade when the imperial invitation came. Constantine called for a worldwide meeting of the Christian church to convene in 325 in the nearby city of Nicaea. He invited every bishop in the known world and told them they could bring a few priests or acolytes each. There were multiple questions on the agenda, the most pressing being how to deal with a theological movement that claimed to be Christian but taught that Jesus wasn't God. There were other questions too: When should we celebrate Easter? Should we ban priests from getting married? Which of our sacred writings are truly inspired by God?

They were important questions, and hundreds of bishops and possibly over a thousand ministers were there weighing in. And this was the first time in history that this many Christian leaders were in the same room.

An interesting and unexpected thing happened during these meetings. There were bishops here, like Nicholas, who had been tortured under Diocletian and refused to recant. And there were others who had denied Christ or sacrificed to Roman gods . . . priests or bishops who had buckled under the threat of violence and incarceration.

Nicholas, who hadn't denied the faith, found that the other priests and bishops wanted to talk to him about it. Nicholas kept getting pulled aside into quiet rooms, shadowed corners, closets and vestibules, where his brother priests would say to him, "Forgive me, when they asked me for a sacrifice, I was afraid, and I sacrificed to the Roman gods" or "They tortured me and I denied Christ."

Wasn't the entire teaching of Christ that God could teach us to love each other and become like Christ?

What these ministers wanted, over and over, was *forgiveness*. Absolution. They wanted to be told that their sin could be washed away.

Nicholas would listen to their stories. Terrible stories about torture, threats, the burning of Scripture, the unpleasant conditions of the prisons. He would listen as his fellow ministers broke down sobbing, desperately ashamed of their weakness, of their failure.

And Nicholas would embrace them, and pray with them, and tell them they were forgiven. Who was he to judge them? Hadn't they all had their moments of weakness? Wasn't the entire teaching of Christ that God could teach us to love each other and become like Christ?

Then he would encourage them to be strong today . . . to be good ministers, to care for the people entrusted into their care, to pray and fast and serve God wholeheartedly.

It was at Nicaea that priests like Nicholas became known as "confessors." They were the ministers who had stayed true in the midst of persecution, the ones you could tell your darkest secrets to and who would assure you of God's forgiveness.

Lord God, help me to remember those times when I have needed forgiveness and received it. Where I still need forgiveness, Lord, please provide it. And help me to be generous to those who need my forgiveness.

18

A PRAYER AGAINST FALSE THEOLOGIES

Things that cause people to stumble are bound to come, but woe to anyone through whom they come. It would be better for them to be thrown into the sea with a millstone tied around their neck than to cause one of these little ones to stumble.

LUKE 17:1-2

There was a theological movement creating confusion and controversy in the church, especially in the eastern parts. A minister named Arius was promoting a theology that claimed that Jesus was not God. He had been created by God, was certainly sent by God, and was unique in creation—had even been made before the beginning of creation—but he was not a divine person.

A good deal of time was set aside at the council to discuss this question. Was Jesus God or not? If Jesus is God's Son, what does that mean? Is it possible that Jesus was created by God?

The tension was high, and tempers ran hot during the conversations. This was all discussed in the context of creating a creed . . . a universally accepted statement of Christian belief that all Christian people could agree on.

There is a story that during these conversations Nicholas became increasingly agitated. The suggestion that Jesus isn't God, and the audacity of these so-called priests to push this strange theology, rankled him.

He wasn't alone. Arius wasn't a bishop, so when the bishops argued about this behind closed doors, it was Eusebius of Nicomedia who represented Arius's ideas. But the bishops often brought Arius into the room to speak for himself, and the majority of bishops in the room found his theology indefensible. And the most passionate, the most outspoken and determined of the theologians were the confessors . . . those who had suffered under Diocletian because they refused to deny the deity of Christ.

And is it any wonder that they would spearhead the objections? Now that Christianity was legal, here was a movement of ministers who would throw away Christ's divinity—and not to avoid prison or escape torture . . . they would throw it away for nothing.

Nicholas, the story goes, became so furious during these conversations that he stood up, still arguing with Arius, and slapped him. This was a shocking and inappropriate moment . . . the whole point of this council was to argue through these things and come to a consensus. But Nicholas was so furious he couldn't contain himself.

He was immediately stripped of his bishop's robe and of his position as a spiritual leader in the church. And since it was illegal to perform an act of violence in the presence of the emperor, Nicholas was thrown in prison.

In all the stories of Nicholas, this was the only moment when he resorted to some sort of violence: slapping Arius when he continued to insist that Jesus wasn't God.

Lord Jesus, there are many people out there who do not know you, or who purposely teach false things about you. Let me be a person who draws others toward the beautiful truths about who you are.

19

A PRAYER FOR BOLDNESS IN SHARING THE GOOD NEWS

Pray also for me, that whenever I speak, words may be given me so that I will fearlessly make known the mystery of the gospel, for which I am an ambassador in chains. Pray that I may declare it fearlessly, as I should.

EPHESIANS 6:19-20

Nicholas found himself in prison (again), only this time thrown in chains by his own brothers. Did he have regrets for his impulsive decision to slap Arius? Or did he see it as something similar to what put him in prison the first time . . . a refusal to reject the clear teachings about Jesus? We don't know for sure.

It seems likely that he may have wondered if he had made a mistake. He had lost not only his freedom but also his vocation. He was no longer a bishop, and he was purposely being kept away from the meetings that were happening elsewhere . . . the largest gathering of Christian leaders in history.

There is a story that we're told about what happened that night. In the story, Nicholas has either a dream or a vision of Jesus appearing to him, alongside his mother, Mary. It must have struck Nicholas that here was a reminder of both the divinity and the humanity of Christ . . . Jesus appearing together with his mother, his only earthly parent.

In some versions of the story, Jesus asks Nicholas why he's in prison, and Nicholas answers, "Because of my love for you." Technically, it's because of the slap, right? But Nicholas sees the slap as a necessary response given the disrespect and falsehood of what Arius was saying to the rest of the assembled bishops.

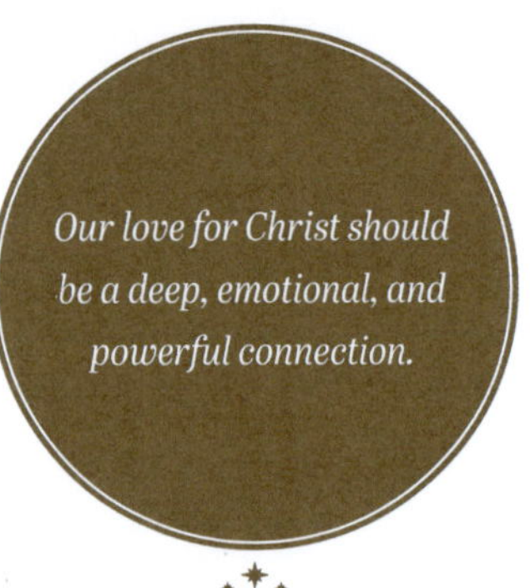

It's said that after this conversation, Jesus gives Nicholas a copy of the gospels, and Mary gives him back his bishop's robes. Come morning, the prison guards arrive to find Nicholas in his bishop's robes, quietly reading Scripture, his chains on the floor beside him.

In some versions of the story, Jesus and Mary don't stop with an appearance to Nicholas. They also go on to talk to Constantine and the other bishops, assuring them that Nicholas should still be in church leadership.

Whatever happened, we do know this: by the end of the Council of Nicaea, Arius's theology had been soundly rejected by nearly the entire gathering (only two bishops refused to sign the Nicaean creed). And Nicholas was still a bishop. He returned to Myra to follow Christ and care for his people there.

The point of this story isn't that we should inflict physical violence on those who don't know Christ well—Nicholas is never again recorded harming anyone, and in fact is often described as both kind and gentle. Rather this story serves as a reminder that our love for Christ should be a deep, emotional, and powerful connection. Our passion for Christ should push us toward action.

Jesus, give me boldness to share the good news about you. Let me know you well and teach others to know you well.

20

A PRAYER TOGETHER WITH ALL THE SAINTS

In him all things were created: things in heaven and on earth, visible and invisible, whether thrones or powers or rulers or authorities; all things have been created through him and for him. He is before all things, and in him all things hold together.

COLOSSIANS 1:16-17

Constantine brought the leaders of the church together to write a statement that all followers of Jesus could agree to. The Christian faith was growing with enormous speed, and as more and more converts joined this new religion, it was having a profound effect on the Roman Empire. Making sure the Christians had clear agreement with one another about the core beliefs of their faith was becoming an issue of state security. Constantine was deeply concerned about this division in the church, and after trying and failing to resolve it quietly and personally with the key leaders of the parties involved, he decided that it was time for the whole church to weigh in.

The question before the church was an important one: Was Jesus God?

Every question of orthodoxy versus heresy comes down to the person and character of God. Who is God? What is God like? And this question was no different. The church leaders set out to write a creed . . . a statement of belief that was clear and a confession of faith for all followers of Jesus.

Even today, this creed remains one that Catholic, Orthodox, and Protestant Christians agree on. Nicholas debated and prayed alongside the other leaders in the room as they painstakingly decided on the words together. In many churches this creed (or some version of it) is said in unison once a week. It was originally written in Greek, so there can be small differences in translation (and this is also why there aren't many sentence breaks!). There were later additions to the creed, most notably to describe the Holy Spirit more fully. But remember, this was a creed that was written in response to a very specific question about who Jesus is.

So they wrote a document to answer that question, a creed that affirmed Jesus is God. He is not a part of creation (in other words, he was not made by God) but rather is the Creator. He is fully God and fully human and became fully human specifically to save us.

And Nicholas was there the first time these words were ever spoken together by the church. The earliest version of the creed, penned in 325, is our prayer for today:

We believe in one God, the Father Almighty,
Maker of all things visible and invisible.

And in one Lord Jesus Christ,
the Son of God,
begotten of the Father
from the essence of the Father,
God from God,
Light from Light,
true God from true God
begotten, not made,
of one substance with the Father,
through whom all things were made,
things in Heaven and things on earth,
who for us, the people,
and for our salvation came down
and took on flesh
and became human;
He suffered,
and rose on the third day,
ascended into heaven,
and will come to judge the living and the dead.

And in the Holy Spirit.

PART FIVE

NICHOLAS IN THE CHRISTIAN EMPIRE

When Nicholas first became a bishop, he was the spiritual leader of a community that was under daily threat of being harmed by the government or the society around it. Christians were a minority, and a persecuted one.

After Constantine became emperor, the church quickly faced a new and perhaps greater challenge: how to remain Christian while dealing with an incredible influx of money, influence, and power.

Constantine kept writing laws that gave Christian leaders more protections and more authority. For instance, he rearranged the financial system of the Roman Empire to direct increasingly large amounts of money toward caring for the poor . . . and handed that money to the churches for distribution.

The Roman centers of worship fell into disrepair as Constantine at first discouraged them, and then later made temple sacrifice illegal. He also began to build Christian churches throughout the empire . . . wisely using his own resources at first and building the churches away from the city centers and current temples. Constantine also invented the idea of "the Holy Land," sponsored churches in Syria Palestine, and encouraged "pilgrimages" to go see the land where Jesus had taught and lived.

And what of Nicholas in these times? As his influence and power grew, he did what he had always done: he gave away his wealth to those in need, and he used what influence he had to protect and lift up the vulnerable and marginalized. Even in the year before his death when a terrible famine came through Asia Minor, the main story we know about him is that he made his way through the city in his seventies, carrying food and money for those who didn't have enough to eat.

We have stories of him interacting with the poorest people in the towns and villages nearby and being on a first-name basis with the leaders and authorities (when he steps in to defend some wrongfully accused prisoners) . . . and even confronting Constantine himself.

Nicholas was interested in following Christ, not in holding on to political power.

21

A PRAYER FOR LIVES OF GODLINESS AND HOLINESS

I urge, then, first of all, that petitions, prayers, intercession and thanksgiving be made for all people—for kings and all those in authority, that we may live peaceful and quiet lives in all godliness and holiness.

1 TIMOTHY 2:1-2

As the Christian faith grew in favor in the empire, the roles and responsibilities of the bishops grew as well. Civic duties began to come to them, at first as invitations, and later as expectations. Nicholas might have been able to sneak away to Bethlehem for a few years back in the old days, but that was no longer the case as he became an increasingly important part of the Roman government.

But Nicholas knew as well as anyone that growing in civic power could corrupt even the most dedicated of Christians. He worked hard to keep his life peaceful, quiet, godly, and holy. And indeed, he was known for these qualities. Many stories of Nicholas start with the people under his care having a problem and then saying that the only person they could turn to was Nicholas himself.

Over and over Nicholas helped turn the hearts of the people around him to the suffering, to the vulnerable, to the hurting. Children, orphans, widows, refugees, the poor.

There are stories of Nicholas intervening in moments of injustice. There's a long and very involved story in which Nicholas realizes that Constantine is demanding too many taxes of his people, and Nicholas journeys to Constantinople to chastise him about it. There are even stories about how pirates would harass the city of Myra and Nicholas was the one called on to deal with them and make them go away.

Throughout these many stories what we see over and over is a man who kept his people at the center of every problem. He never swooped in and just pronounced a theological truth that everyone must follow. He never exerted his authority and said, "You must do what I say because I am the bishop." Over and over Nicholas helped turn the hearts of the people around him to the suffering, to the vulnerable, to the hurting. Children, orphans, widows, refugees, the poor.

And while there are supernatural miracles attributed to Nicholas, the most common and best-known miracles are the ones that come from his heart of love: stories about the man who would throw his own money in through a window to keep people from slavery. The man who would confront the emperor about overtaxation. The man who would buy a rug from a poor man and then return the rug to the man's wife.

Nicholas was not a man focused on power. He was not a man concerned about gaining authority. He didn't care for riches or influence.

Instead, he focused on being a man of peace. He was concerned about living a quiet life. He cared about godliness and holiness.

Who wouldn't want a spiritual leader like that?

Lord God, I know that each of us is called to places of influence. There are people who look up to me, who see me as an example in their spiritual lives. Please shape me to be a person of peace, living a quiet life. Teach me how to be godly. Help me to grow in holiness.

22

A PRAYER FOR THE MOST VULNERABLE

Religion that God our Father accepts as pure and faultless is this: to look after orphans and widows in their distress and to keep oneself from being polluted by the world.

JAMES 1:27

Another traditional story about Nicholas comes to us in the Middle Ages, told in many different ways. In some versions it involves scholars, in others children. In some there is murder involved, in others just thievery. And in a few versions those who commit the crime are punished, while in most they get advice from Nicholas about how to live a better life, and end up making an honest living selling pickles!

Here's the one I find most interesting:

In this version, there are three children. Three small boys are lost in the city, and they ask a butcher if there is "room in the inn" . . . does he have a place they can stay the night? And at first he says no, because things are difficult everywhere. There's a famine going on, and people are short of money and the butcher can barely find meat to sell. But his wife whispers in his ear and together they come up with a grotesque plan. They chop up the children and put them in a barrel full of brine so they can sell the meat as pork.

But Saint Nicholas comes along and asks to stay in the butcher's home. The butcher can't turn away a holy man. He asks Nicholas if he'd like something to eat, and everything he offers Nicholas refuses. Then Nicholas points out the evil barrel and says he'd like whatever is in there. The butcher is terrified, but when he opens the barrel, the children are alive and whole.

In fact, there is a famous French children's song ("Complainte des Enfants au Saloir") that tells this whole story, and it is the children who have the last word. When they "wake up," they say, "I had such a good sleep!" and "Me too!" and "I thought I was in paradise!"

There are some things about this story that I think capture the heart of Nicholas in beautiful ways, even if it's a later addition to his stories. One, Nicholas believes in the power of God to transform even the worst situation. He has a bold confidence that God can solve any problem.

Two, I love that in most versions of this story the evil murderers are forgiven in some way. The children aren't dead anymore, so Nicholas uses their death and resurrection to shame the evildoers and turn their life toward good. Nicholas believed in the power of forgiveness.

Three, the heart of Nicholas for the innocent and the youth is on full display. In times of trouble in our world, it's often children who are the most vulnerable and most easily taken advantage of by others. Nicholas cared about the vulnerable.

Lord God, in these times when people take advantage of children and harm them for their own personal gain, we pray for your power to notice the vulnerable, and we ask you to empower us to right the wrongs done against them.

23

A PRAYER FOR THE WRONGFULLY ACCUSED

The wicked flee though no one pursues,
but the righteous are as bold as a lion.

PROVERBS 28:1

One of the oldest written stories of Nicholas goes like this:

When Nicholas was the influential bishop of Myra, there was a riot near the harbor. Some thieves—pretending to be Roman soldiers—were stealing food from local vendors. The furious people formed a mob and soon were threatening not only the thieves but also the very soldiers who had been impersonated.

The crowd grew so loud that Nicholas could hear the commotion, and he walked down to the harbor to see what was happening. When he got to the bottom of it, he calmed the crowds and invited the true soldiers to come and eat with him.

On their way back to his home, some of the townspeople stopped him and said, "Nicholas, if only you hadn't been so distracted by this riot, you would have seen that three men were wrongfully accused of crimes they didn't commit . . . and even now the executioner is ready to drop the sword on their necks."

Nicholas had walked to see what was happening at the riot, but at this news he sprinted to the place where the beheading would take place. He arrived to see the three men on their knees, hooded, waiting for the blade to fall. Nicholas ran directly to the executioner and snatched the sword from his hand.

When the praeses—the provincial governor—heard what had happened, he confronted Nicholas about why he thought he could intervene in a state execution. Nicholas marveled that a man caught in the evil act of killing innocents would confront him and called him a "sacrilegious blood shedder," promising to report him to the emperor himself.

Terrified, the praeses fell to his knees and told Nicholas he had been ordered to kill these men—regardless of their innocence—by the heads of state, Eudoxius and Simonides. It turns out they had been bribed with a great deal of silver. "It is not Eudoxius and Simonides who did this, but silver and gold," Nicholas said, disgusted with the entire event.

The soldiers begged Nicholas not to report the praeses to the emperor, for they were men under authority, too, and explained that he had been forced into the situation. After hearing the soldiers' argument, and after strong promises that this would never happen again, Nicholas agreed.

After all of this, Nicholas took the soldiers back to his home, and together they ate and drank. The soldiers were filled with wonder that this religious man was so bold . . . that he would intervene with government officials who had the power to condemn him to death.

God, give me boldness to intervene when the state does the wrong thing. Let me be an advocate for the wrongfully accused and the unjustly incarcerated. Let my hand stop the sword from killing the innocent, through the certainty of your power. For you are greater than all the governments of this world, and I am your representative.

24

A PRAYER FOR EVERYTHING AND EVERYONE

The angel said to them, "Do not be afraid. I bring you good news that will cause great joy for all the people."

LUKE 2:10

Nicholas had a way of making everyone around him know that he loved them, that he cared for them, and that when they had problems, he would be looking for solutions. He was beloved by children, because he saw them and responded to them. He was beloved by young women, who saw him as an advocate. Sailors adored him, and Nicholas would often head down to the docks and pray a blessing over departing ships.

Over time Nicholas became the patron saint of many people and places . . . too many to list. He's the patron saint of bakers and bankers, barrel makers and brewers. Newlyweds and single women, orphans and pirates, murderers and judges. Pharmacists and priests, prostitutes, poets, and preachers all claim him.

Seven countries, hundreds of towns, and thousands of churches worldwide look to Nicholas as their patron. And why?

Because he took care of orphans and widows. He prayed for sailors and watched over children. He made sure that young women were protected. He helped thieves to repent and find a better life. He cared for the poor.

It's telling that the most famous story of the historical Saint Nicholas isn't a miraculous event. It's not him appearing in a dream, or a sudden healing, or even the calming of the sea. I'm guessing many people reading this book had never heard those kinds of stories about him before.

May the Lord bring us more people like Nicholas. May God teach us to be those people.

The most famous, the most well-known story, is Nicholas throwing gold through a window (or down a chimney or putting it in the family shoes). It's a story about seeing a need and using the resources he had to solve the need. It's the wonder of love, the marvel of caring for others. It's the miracle of kindness.

It's no wonder that he has become so inextricably linked with Christmas. Nicholas cared for everyone and brought joy to everyone. He brought Christ into every conversation, every situation, in a way that made people feel loved, championed, cared for. And whether they were in the middle of famine, illness, or war, political upheaval or persecution, Nicholas understood. He had been there, he had experienced that, and he responded with understanding, kindness, and a commitment to using everything at his disposal to bring what was needed: food, healing, strength, patience, money, or prayers.

And Nicholas understood something that many of us are prone to forget: the coming of Christ is not something to fear, is not something that should fill us with terror. The good news of the arrival of Christ is something that should bring joy and celebration. Indeed, that's what we celebrate at Christmastime. Nicholas was someone who brought that joy of Christ's arrival into the everyday.

May the Lord bring us more people like Nicholas. May God teach us to be those people.

Lord God, teach me to be like Nicholas. Open my eyes to the people around me—waiters and landlords and grocery clerks and coworkers, family and neighbors, politicians and the poor—and give me insight into their needs, their deep desires, and the ways I can bring your love and holy kindness into their lives. May I be a messenger of your joyous arrival. Let me see all people through your eyes, and let my hands be your hands, working in service to your will.

25

A PRAYER FOR PEACE ON EARTH AND GOODWILL TOWARD ALL PEOPLE

Suddenly a great company of the heavenly host appeared with the angel, praising God and saying, "Glory to God in the highest heaven, and on earth peace to those on whom his favor rests."

LUKE 2:13-14

December 25, 336, was the very first Christmas. For the Romans, December 25 had been called *Dies Natalis Solis Invicti*, or the "Birthday of the Invincible Sun" because it was the date of the longest night of the year. But Constantine decreed that it would now commemorate the birth of Jesus, who was the true "Sun of Righteousness." And so the Christian church in Rome held a service to celebrate the birth of Jesus on December 25.

And the next year, more churches celebrated. And the next, still more. Old Saint Nicholas, racked with arthritis but still serving as bishop, was alive to see the first seven Christmases and died just short of his eighth . . . on December 6, 343.

Christmas had already started to pull in traditions from other holidays. Saturnalia was in December, too, and one

Saturnalia tradition was to give small gifts to children. It quickly became a Christmas tradition as well.

As the holiday grew and changed, Nicholas became a more and more important part of it. Why do we give gifts to children? Maybe because the wise men gave gifts to Jesus. Or maybe because Saint Nicholas loved children and brought them little gifts in celebration of Christ's birthday . . . in their stockings hung by the fire, or in their shoes, or under their pillows.

In time, of course, the stories of Nicholas would shift into a legend of a jolly old man in a red coat, shooting around the world to magically appear down chimneys and eat milk and cookies and give good children good things. There's something wonderful about that.

Glory to you, God,
in the highest heaven,
and may there be peace on
earth, and your goodwill
toward all people.

But I prefer to think of the old man who gets up before the sun has risen on Christmas morning. He gets dressed, eats his humble breakfast, shuffles along while feeling the pain of the arthritis in his back. He rubs his broken nose and makes his way into the chapel, where he lowers his aching knees before the altar as he prays.

He lights the candles for the service to come. Outside, he hears the familiar sounds of the city of Myra waking up—the livestock, parents calling to their children, sailors shouting at the distant docks.

He remembers his childhood friends in Patara, running with them past the temples of Apollo and Artemis, now in disrepair. He used to go with his parents to visit the sick, he remembers that. So many sick, now gone. He remembers the warmth of his uncle's eyes when he first became a priest and the cold stone floor of the prison. He remembers the storm on the way to Bethlehem, and how his prayer for peace on the sea was miraculously answered.

He reflects on the cave in Bethlehem, where the God of the universe became a human being, God from God, Light from Light, True God from True God.

"Glory to God in the highest heaven," he says, half a reminder to himself and half a prayer. "And on earth peace to those on whom his favor rests."

He thinks of the children in his city—and the children of the world—and desperately prays for God's peace. No more war, no more disease, no more fighting, or grief, or pain. *God protect those little ones.* He can hear them now, laughing, as they run ahead of their parents toward the church.

He throws open the doors and lets the children and the sunlight in.

Glory to you, God, in the highest heaven, and may there be peace on earth, and your goodwill toward all people. Amen.

Conclusion

SAINT NICHOLAS TO THE WHOLE WORLD

When Nicholas died, his body was interred in his own church in Myra. Over the years, people traveled to visit the church and pay their respects to Nicholas. This included sailors who would come from all over the world on their various business trips, who might stop in while at port. They took his story back home with them, and more people would come to see Nicholas.

In 1087, three ships full of merchants from Bari, Italy, stopped in Myra. The Roman Empire was long gone, and the Seljuk Empire now ruled the area. The merchants were shown where Nicholas's bones lay. The local monks were suspicious of the merchants, and their suspicions were confirmed when they discovered the merchants breaking into the tomb that night with an iron bar.

Nicholas became "Saint Nicholas" because Christians agreed, "This is a person who followed Jesus well, we can learn from him."

Legends say the entire town of Myra chased the men to their ship. They escaped, and on May 9, 1087, the bones of Nicholas arrived in Bari, Italy. A crypt was built to house the relics, completed two years later in October of 1089, and later a magnificent church was constructed on that spot. Nicholas became one of the most influential saints in medieval Europe, and many of our Christmas traditions are handed down through that lens.

Every follower of Jesus is a saint. But in many Christian traditions there's a special category of saint: those brothers and sisters who have set an extraordinary example for the rest of us in how to follow Jesus well and thus end up with "saint" as part of their name. Nicholas became "Saint Nicholas" because Christians agreed, "This is a person who followed Jesus well, we can learn from him."

All of this from a Greek orphan boy who cared deeply for the poor, who saw those in need and worked hard to meet those needs. While he likely wouldn't care much about magnificent buildings with his name on them, no doubt he would be pleased to see that his lasting legacy—a millennium and a half after his death—is to give children gifts in his name.

I love Christmas. The flying reindeer and the magic of the old elf who can fly around the entire world in a night is wonderful. But I am honestly more moved by the fact that every December there are millions of people around the world who stay up late to wrap gifts and tuck them under a tree, or into some shoes, or drop them in a stocking. In some countries there are traditions on the Feast of Saint Nicholas of going door to door and collecting money for the poor. And there are these Christmas moments when we stop and remind ourselves to be patient with our friends and family, or to be more generous, or to take time to tell someone how much we care for them. "It's Christmas, after all."

As we move toward a new year, my hope and my prayer is that I could take that Christmas spirit forward with me. I want to celebrate Christmas every day, to be more loving and generous to the people around me. To remember that God has promised peace on earth and goodwill toward humanity. To see the needs of people clearly, like Nicholas did, and become a miracle of God in their lives. And that is my prayer for you, dear reader, as well.

Lord Jesus, as we celebrate Saint Nicholas, remind us that he was an ordinary person who became beloved around the world and throughout time by doing two things: loving you and loving the people around him. Teach us also to be your loving miracle to the people we see in need around us. Amen.

Timeline

- March 15, AD 270—Nicholas is born in Patara.
- 300—Nicholas becomes bishop in Myra.
- 303—Diocletian orders the destruction of Christian Scriptures and church buildings and the arrest of all Christian leaders who wouldn't recant or make sacrifices to the Roman gods.
- 303–308 (?)—Nicholas spends several years in prison because of his faith.
- May 1, 305—Diocletian steps down as emperor, his poor health making him too weak to continue.
- July 25, 306—After the death of his father, Constantine is acclaimed as emperor by the soldiers in his army.

- December 3, 311—Diocletian dies.
- November 1, 312—Constantine has a vision of a cross in the sky and converts to Christianity.
- February 313—Constantine's Edict of Milan promises religious freedom in the Empire and specifically grants civil equality to Christians.
- 312–315—Nicholas spends three years in Egypt and Syria Palestine, mostly living in a cave near Bethlehem.
- July 3, 324—Constantine becomes sole ruler of the Roman Empire.
- May–July 325—Nicholas attends the Council of Nicaea, the first "worldwide" Christian gathering. The council was formed to create solutions for a number of difficult issues facing the Christian community.
- 325—Lycia becomes its own province, with Myra as capital city, making Nicholas's role as bishop instantly more influential and important.
- 333–335—A terrible famine rages through Asia Minor, and Nicholas spearheads taking care of the people using the resources of the church (and by miraculously procuring grain from some sailors).

- December 25, 336—Constantine declares the first Christmas in Rome.
- December 6, 343—Nicholas passes away, beloved by all who knew him, at the age of seventy-three.

The 100 Percent True, Completely Historical Story of Saint Nicholas

It's only natural to wonder, which of those amazing stories are true? Which are history, and which are legends or myths?

It's a complicated question. A lot of the written works of the church in this era were destroyed during the persecutions, especially in the area where Nicholas lived and worked. We don't have a single document that Nicholas himself wrote, and some of the stories about him—which may be true!—weren't written down for years . . . sometimes even hundreds of years.

Adding to the confusion, there was another Nicholas (Nicholas of Sion) who lived about two hundred years after our Nicholas, was probably named after him, was born in the same region, was also a bishop, and died in December. In later years their stories sometimes got mixed together, and so some stories about Nicholas are actually about Nicholas, if you know what I mean.

Then there are questions about what could be "true" that comes down to a very personal decision about whether you believe in miracles and if so, what kind. So, for instance, we might look at an older Nicholas story where he confronts Constantine about taxes and miraculously sends word to a distant town faster than is humanly possible. Some might say it's "based on a true story" that Nicholas thought taxes were too much, but the miracle part didn't really happen. Someone else might insist the miracle did happen, and it's basically decided by whether you believe that kind of miracle is likely to have taken place.

Here's a quick list of some of the most and least likely "historical" Nicholas facts (from my point of view, anyway):

THINGS THAT ARE HISTORICALLY ACCURATE

(or pretty close anyway)

Nicholas was born in Patara to wealthy Greek parents who (tradition tells us) were named Theophanes and Nona. They died when he was young, and he sold everything and became a priest. He later became bishop of Myra. He went to visit Egypt and lived in a cave near Bethlehem for three years. The traditional dates for that journey have been handed down through the centuries by the religious community he stayed with in those years, a community that is still in that location. His birth and death dates are almost certainly in the right ballpark.

The oldest (written) Nicholas story is about the bishop racing to save the people who are about to be wrongfully executed. The details (the names of the local Roman government officials) as well as the date of the account (within sixty years of Nicholas's death) argue some version of this story happened "in real life."

The story of throwing gold coins to save the young women from slavery is likewise an old one that didn't change much over the years, and it is both very likely to be true and in many ways the heart of the Nicholas story.

Lastly, because we have his bones in Bari, Italy, and because a doctor was allowed to study those bones in the 1950s, we know that Nicholas's nose was broken at some point (we don't know how—he could have stepped on a rake for all we know), and that he had terrible arthritis in his later life.

THINGS THAT SEEM VERY LIKELY

It is almost certain that Nicholas was thrown in prison during the rule of Diocletian, along with all the bishops in that area and at that time. The tradition is that he was in prison for five years, which is pretty long given what we know about Diocletian's policies, but not impossible. Tradition has always said that Nicholas was a "confessor" . . . one of those who refused to deny Jesus. This would make sense if he was kept in prison that long!

THINGS THAT SEEM MORE LIKELY THAN NOT

There's some debate about Nicholas being at the Council of Nicaea, and also about whether he slapped Arius. The oldest (and shortest) lists of those in attendance don't have Nicholas's name, but we know those are incomplete. The longer lists all record Nicholas in attendance. The arguments against the longer lists are partly historical (they're not as old as the short lists), partly theological (different parts of the church were caretakers of the different records), and partly skepticism (the number of people on the longer lists seem like the names might have been chosen to have "numerical significance" rather than accuracy). On the other hand, most of the ministers in attendance were the Eastern bishops, the timing is right for Nicholas to be there, and Nicaea would have been a relatively easy journey from Myra.

As for the slap, some people argue that's why Nicholas isn't listed in attendance (either out of shame for his actions or because he had been removed as a bishop as a result of the slap). Some argue Arius wasn't a bishop and therefore wasn't personally in the room with the bishops, and the earliest account says Nicholas slapped "a certain Arian," not necessarily Arius himself.

As for me, the story rings true, the dates and location all work, and while I don't love the idea of Nicholas smacking someone, even the most saintly among us are real human beings with passions and moments of frustration. Whether historical or not, it's a good reminder that the doctrine that

Jesus is God was an emotional, important piece of theology in the church . . . and it's easy to imagine that Nicholas—who refused to denounce the deity of Jesus in prison—might have some strong opinions about other people throwing that away for nothing.

STORIES THAT ARE PRETTY UNLIKELY TO BE HISTORICAL

There are a number of stories that magically appear in medieval Europe about Nicholas, and many of those stories have medieval themes and even sometimes medieval settings. A great example included in this book is the story of the three boys cut to pieces in the barrels. The versions of the story are pretty vastly different (three boys or three university scholars, for instance) and even the ending of the story is different. Sometimes Nicholas helps the evil innkeepers (or butchers) start a pickle business, or sometimes he forgives them. The stories feel like medieval stories, show up in medieval times, and seem to spread quickly with little tweaks by different medieval authors.

The story of Nicholas praying for the storm to be still is one of those that's all mixed up with Nicholas of Sion. But it's a story that I love and decided to include. Having said that, anyone on a boat in a storm has probably prayed for it to stop, and God answers prayers the way God chooses.

Regardless, I do think these stories are still useful. They keep pushing us to consider the core ideals of Nicholas:

justice, care for the poor, love for our neighbor, trust in God, giving gifts to those in need. Some stories might not be historical but could still have truth woven into them.

THINGS WE JUST DON'T KNOW

Was Nicholas married? Maybe. A lot of priests were in those days, and it's not uncommon for women to be erased from the historical narratives of the time.

Who were his friends? His enemies? Would he have liked cookies and could he digest milk? We just don't know.

STORIES THAT DIDN'T HAPPEN

(but are still a lot of fun)

Nicholas never asked a reindeer with a shiny nose to guide his sleigh through the foggy night. Nicholas lived in a time of occasional famine and food shortages and almost certainly did not have a belly like a bowl full of jelly. He probably never adopted an orphan named Buddy who crawled into his bag of toys. But even these stories are still somehow connected back to Nicholas: he would do whatever it took to get people what they needed. He was known as a person who brought plenty in times of famine. He loved orphans and took care of them. So even the stories that are furthest away from historical truth still have the stamp of Nicholas on them.

Bibliography

If you want to learn more about Nicholas, here are some great books and stories to check out:

Glahn, Sandra L. *Nobody's Mother: Artemis of the Ephesians in Antiquity and the New Testament.* IVP Academic, 2023. A great theological and historical overview of information about Artemis of the Ephesians.

Marek, Christian. *In the Land of a Thousand Gods: A History of Asia Minor in the Ancient World.* In Collaboration with Peter Frei. Translated by Steven Rendall. Princeton University Press, 2018. A wonderful, readable, fascinating history about the world of Asia Minor in the time of Nicholas.

Methodius ad Theodorum (probably Patriarch Methodius I of Constantinople). *The Life of Saint Nicholas of Myra*. Translated by Roger Pearse. https://www.stnicholascenter.org/who-is-st-nicholas/stories-legends/classic-sources/methodius-ad-theodorum.

Michael the Archimandrite. "The Life of Saint Nicholas the Wonderworker." St. Nicholas Center. https://www.stnicholascenter.org/who-is-st-nicholas/stories-legends/classic-sources/michael-the-archimandrite. This is the oldest complete biography of Nicholas we have, from the ninth century. It pulls together many legends of Nicholas from over the centuries, and—like most of the early Nicholas content—is a specifically religious biography.

St. Nicholas Center. "*Praxis de Tributo* or The Tax Miracle of Nicholas of Myra." https://www.stnicholascenter.org/who-is-st-nicholas/stories-legends/classic-sources/praxis-de-tributo-400-900. Another anonymous Greek account of Nicholas.

St. Nicholas Center. "*Stratelatis* or The Military Officers." https://www.stnicholascenter.org/who-is-st-nicholas/stories-legends/classic-sources/istratelatis. This is the earliest account of Nicholas we have (about AD 400) and is a partial chapter in Greek of a larger work about Nicholas.

There are a number of other ancient sources, but many of them are either compilations of the sources above, translations, or retellings. Having said that, I read a lot of them! If you want to read them for yourself, the St. Nicholas Center has a full online collection (translated into English). The St. Nicholas Center is definitely the most comprehensive and accessible place to learn about Nicholas! Check it out at stnicholascenter.org.

Acknowledgments

A good number of my books would not exist without the wisdom, kindness, and intelligence of Sarah Atkinson. She has been a trusted and faithful companion in my publishing career, and I am so thankful for her warmth, generosity, and friendship. Merry Christmas, Sarah, and a hearty ho ho hoooooooo to you and your family.

Wes Yoder, my agent and trusted friend, has likewise been integral in bringing this and all of my books to life. I am so thankful for the years we have spent together working on these books. I've often said that one of my favorite things about becoming an author is the many friends God has blessed me with on the journey, and Wes is top of that list!

Debbie King was my editor for this book and just did an amazing job, helping me say things with clarity and accuracy, and translating my undiluted excitement for the story of Nicholas into words that made sense to someone who wasn't immersed in nonstop Nicholas study. She also taught me how to spell several words correctly, including *Nicaea*, which you'd think I would have picked up in seminary. I am so thankful for Debbie's keen eye, kind corrections, and excellent suggestions.

I'd like to thank our copy editors, Lisanne Kaufmann and Cheryl Warner, who caught my many typos and careless mistakes and all around made this book better.

I'm also so in love with this beautiful cover, designed by Ron Kaufmann. Thank you, Ron, and thanks to Kaylee Small who took my very long and rambling email about covers and helped the design team turn it into something beautiful.

Thank you also to Mary Campbell, acquisitions editor and traffic director, who has been keeping the quality high on everything as it comes through. Thanks to Michelle Polsley, our resident marketer. You probably have this book in your hands right now because of her hard work. And also huge thanks to Laura Cruise, who did the interior design on the book. Literally every page you've read has Laura's excellent work represented on it.

As always, thanks to my family, near and extended, who continually make Christmas my favorite holiday and have managed the last year of unsolicited Nicholas stories with patience and good cheer.

And finally, dear readers, to you. May the stories of Nicholas draw you closer to Christ and one another. Peace to you!

About the Author

MATT MIKALATOS is an author and former missionary who lives in the Portland, Oregon, area with his wife and three daughters. He's the coauthor of *Praying with Saint Patrick* (with Aaron Burns) and the award-winning *Loving Disagreement* (with Kathy Khang).